SIMPLY
REVELATION

*A Simple Look at a
Complicated Book*

THERESA J. ROYAL

SIMPLY
REVELATION

A Simple Look at a Complicated Book

THERESA J. ROYAL

HUNTER ENTERTAINMENT NETWORK

Colorado Springs, Colorado

Simply Revelation

To order products, or for any other correspondence:

Hunter Entertainment Network
4164 Austin Bluffs Parkway, Suite 214
Colorado Springs, Colorado 80918
Tel. (253) 906-2160
E-mail: contact@hunter-entertainment.com
Or reach us on the internet: www.hunter-entertainment.com

"Offering God's Heart to a Dying World"

This book and all other Hunter Heart Publishing™ and Hunter Heart Kids™ books and products are available at Christian bookstores and distributors worldwide.

Chief Editor: Gord Dormer

Creative design: Phil Coles Independent Design
Cover format and logos: Exousia Marketing Group www.exousiamg.com

ISBN: 978-1-937741-38-9
For Worldwide Distribution, Printed in the United States of America.

Acknowledgments

Again, I thank my Ladies' Sunday School Class and others who have earnestly prayed for me as I penned this book. I could feel their prayers each time I hit a brick wall. Eldon Martin's help with the computer was invaluable, as I still have so many problems with my Computer Illiteracy. Eldon and Lisa also read the book to see if it was correct scripturally. Cynthia Rodriguez also read it to see if it was simple enough for the average Christian to understand. Kay Siegler helped me save all the material on my memory chip and changed a few things when I could not do it myself.

I want to thank my publisher and company who put it all together. Their help has been greatly appreciated. Most of all as usual, I want to thank the Lord for putting in my mind what I needed to write. He, again, authored this book; I merely typed it for Him. If there are any errors they are mine, if any conviction on the reader's part, that comes from the Lord.

Table of Contents

Introduction

In the beginning, we find the apostle John on the Isle of Patmos, a penal colony, where he has been exiled due to his faithful preaching of the Word of God. Was he filled with self-pity, having a pity patter party, feeling sorry for himself? Was he depressed having been a victim for obeying his Lord? No, it says clearly he was in the Spirit on the Lord's Day. He had been worshipping Jesus for who He was and what He had done. In other words, his eyes were not on his circumstances, he was captivated by his Lord, in deep ecstasy of worship. No wonder God had chosen John to give this revelation of Himself, as a record for us today.

The author of this book was the apostle John who also wrote the gospel of John and books I, II, and III of John. Jesus told him to write all down that he saw, as he was given these startling visions of the future. One has to put themselves in John's place in 95 AD to understand what a shock these visions were to him. After all he had never seen a car, train, plane, radio, rocket, or T.V., or even heard of the technology we, and especially our young people, have been exposed to today. Many of my generation born in the 1930's or even before, have grappled with this book, especially when we first read it. Today, we understand it much more clearly. Part of this is due to our need today to understand the vital message it brings.

Revelation
Chapters 1-22

01 REVELATION
The Revelation of Jesus Christ

Early in the first chapter, we see in 1:3 that there is a three-fold promise given to all who read, hear, and keep that which is written in this book. When God makes a promise, He keeps it. John was told here by the angel the time was near. If it was near then, you will see by many of the signs, that not only are we in the last days of the church age, but the Rapture is very near. It is definitely nearer than ever and we all must be ready. We dare not think because He has delayed, He will not act. God is sometimes slow, but He is sure.

John was told to send a copy of the writings to the seven churches in Asia. These were actual churches, but were symbolic of churches down throughout the ages as well. Each church today is represented by one of these churches. His salutation to them was grace and peace sent by the Holy Spirit (#7 denotes completeness, perfection). The perfect Holy Spirit was there before the throne and Jesus Christ the faithful witness. He was the first born from the dead, and ruler of all rulers of the earth (John breaks out in praise). "To Him (Jesus) who loved us and washed us from our sins in His own blood and made us kings and priests to His God and Father, to Him be the glory and dominion forever and ever. (This refers to the resurrection of Jesus at Calvary; death could not hold Him in the grave.)

The coming in the clouds in (1:7) is of the 2nd Coming not the Rapture. In the Rapture believers, the church, are caught up to meet Jesus in the clouds. In the 2nd Coming, Jesus will actually set His feet upon the earth when He comes in the clouds. He will set up His thousand year reign and every eye shall see Him. Most scholars believe the Rapture will take place before the Tribulation, between chapters 3 and 4, due to the fact the Church is never mentioned again, and God's character, which is not to pass judgment till He has removed His children first. This will be for believers in the church age only. At this time, they will go before the Judgment Seat of Christ and be judged for rewards. (2 Corinthians 5:10, 1 Corinthians 3:8) We will share more on judgments later in this book. All the lost of the ages will be judged at the Great White Throne Judgment.

The Alpha and the Omega in v.8 are the first and last letters of the Greek alphabet to show Jesus is omnipresent, He has unlimited existence. He has always been in the past, is now, and will forever be in the future. John, a Christian brother, and a fellow persecuted Christian, was on the Isle of Patmos for his exercising his faith. He had been confined for sharing the Word of God and the testimony of Jesus Christ. He heard a loud voice (Jesus' voice) like a trumpet, (clear and distinguishable) telling him to write down in a book what He saw and was told.

John saw seven golden lamp stands (symbolic of seven churches, and churches throughout the ages) with Jesus in the midst of them. (Jesus is always in the midst of His churches.) He was dressed regally (Daniel 7:9 description as God the Father, Jesus is co-equal with God Hebrews 1:3) and His head and hair were white as snow (This denotes His purity). His eyes like a flame of fire and His feet were like brass (This tells us He has now come to judge, not tender and meek like a lamb). His voice was as the sound of many waters (powerful) and He held in His hand the seven stars (This symbolized the pastors; no one could get to them without first going through Him). Out of His mouth came a double-edged sword and His countenance was like the sun shining in its strength. He created the earth by His Spoken Word, and He will destroy it with the same Powerful Spoken Word.

John fell at Jesus' feet as dead, he was so afraid. This was a fearful vision, but Jesus told him not to fear. He was told not to be afraid for He was the First and the Last and the One who had the Keys to Hades and Death. We also have nothing to fear in this world, only He is to be feared. Then John was told again to write down all that he had seen, the things that are and would take place after this. He then explained the lamp stands are the churches and the angels are the pastors of these churches.

02 REVELATION
Letters to the Churches Part I

Jesus personally dictated a letter to each of the pastors of the seven churches. These were actual churches in Asia and are representative of all churches throughout history and of today. He praised each of them for the positives and pointed out their problems where there was change needed. He then gave them a prescription to correct the problems.

Ephesus was a commercial, political religious center located on the Aegean Sea and the first letter was written to them. A temple of Diana, a fertility goddess was there. Paul ministered there three years and laid a strong foundation and he wrote the book of Ephesians to this church. Through the years, this church became large and proud. Jesus first described Himself as the One who holds all the churches and their pastors in His strong right hand. This should bring comfort to any pastor as no one can harm them but by going through Him first. He is not a God who stands far off, for He made it clear He knew about their work, labor, patience, and their intolerance of evil. They even tested those who just made claims to be, but were counterfeit apostles. He also praised them that they didn't grow weary from well-doing. (Galatians 6:9)

There was one problem. In all that good religious activity, they had forgotten the most important thing, their first love (Their intimate relationship with Jesus Christ). How easy it would be for a church like this to get in this shape. Busyness, having religious activity, can be substituted so easily for an intimate relationship with the Lord. Our God loves us too much to let this happen. He will never allow this to happen without reminding us, like He did to the church, to remember from where they had fallen, and repent and return back to Him. He stressed the fact they hated the deeds of the Nicolaitans (Compromisers). But He clearly stressed they needed to open their spiritual ears and hear what His Spirit was saying. He warned them He would remove their usefulness and their success if they didn't re-evaluate and return to their former passion for souls and for Him. He wanted them to become faithful and not drift from their love for Him. Anyone who loves anything above their love for Jesus is an idol worshipper, and will not eat from the Tree of Life (Have eternal life).

The second church Jesus dictated a letter to was the church in Smyrna, located 25 miles north of Ephesus. It had an excellent harbor in the Aegean Sea and it was known as a port of Asia. A strong group of Jews opposed to Christianity was there, plus a strong Roman group who worshipped the emperor. Much persecution came from these two groups. Jesus described Himself as the First and the Last who was dead and came to life. Again Jesus made it clear that He knew all about them, their work, affliction, their economical poverty, (though they were rich spiritually,) and the blasphemy they endured from the Jews, who were really ruled by Satan.

Unfortunately, there are many today who have the same rule of Satan in their lives. The persecution that is happening, and will get worse, came from the Master Deceiver, Satan himself. How good it is to hear the truth spoken and not someone who tries to be politically correct. Jesus told them though they would endure tribulation, it would be for a short time (ten days). The challenge was to be faithful until death and they had the promise of life eternal and the second (spiritual) death cannot harm them. The tribulation is temporary, but eternal life is forever. Jesus never had anything to condemn in this church. We are seeing less and less of this type of church today.

John wrote this third letter by direction to the pastor (angel) of the church at Pergamum, which was located sixty miles north of Smyrna. As normal, it was signed at the beginning by Jesus who called Himself He who has the sharp two-edged sword. (He referred to the Word of God piercing the hearts of man.) He told them He knew their works and where they dwelt. He called it the place where Satan ruled from. It was no wonder Jesus called it that for it was the center of four pagan cults. They worshipped Zeus, Athena, Dionysus, and Esclepius in Pergamum. Also, the government demanded emperor worship.

They did not compromise with the false teachings. Their faith still remained strong. Yet, the Lord did have something against them. Some in their midst held to the doctrine of Balaam who compromised their faith with two sensual appeals. One was eating meat that had been offered to idols, (probably discounted) and committed sexual immorality. This was not merely a difference of opinion, but heresy. God had told them what He expected. Though they were obedient in staying faithful in other matters, they were committing this untruth and some even followed the doctrine of the Nicolaitans, which also tolerated licentious, compromise, and sexual immorality.

This has always been a snare of the devil and most certainly is today. Most of the churches today have ceased preaching on this that society, as a whole, has embraced with terrible consequences. What one generation tolerates, the next one will accept. It began to happen and in one generation, it was accepted with a great exodus of the church by youth and young adults. Now, no one even mentions this sin anymore, especially since our government threatens churches with the removal of their tax exemption. You get a crowd if you compromise and many huge churches are so because they never mention this sin. Jesus hated this, and still does.

Jesus issued a challenge to this church, repent and He would come with the Word, which was being neglected in this matter. Open your spiritual ears to what the Holy Spirit says in this letter. He made two promises to them if they would do this, hidden manna would be given, and they would receive a white stone, which was what a defendant in a court received if he was found not guilty. He would have a new name, a new identity. Only the Lord can give us the identity of one found not guilty, by His becoming our substitute sacrifice.

The fourth church John was to send a letter to from Jesus was the church at Thyatira. He signed it as the Son of God describing Himself with two symbols of judgment, fire and brass. Jesus knew all about their deeds, as well. Among His praise was for their love, service, faith, patience, and works. With all this praise, they perhaps thought He surely could not find anything wrong with their church, but we know good works do not nullify sins.

What Jesus had against this church was the fact they had tolerated a woman who called herself Jezebel, a false prophet. She not only taught sexual immorality was alright, but she seduced them into that practice. She also tolerated them eating meat sacrificed to idols. He had given her time to repent, but she had not. So, He said He would cast her in a bed of sickness and those who participated with her would also suffer the consequences of their sin, bringing great tribulation into their life. In other words, they would suffer for their sins. Judgment often is directly associated with the sin committed. How many today are suffering the consequences of their immorality with AIDS, herpes, and many sexually transmitted diseases that are returning with a vengeance, where they had nearly been wiped out with modern day antibiotics. Today, they are resisting these same medications, as the strains get worse.

But still like here at Thyatira, they chose to close their spiritual ears to preaching of "Be sure your sins will find you out." (Numbers 32:23) Romans 6:23 says, "The wages of sin is death" (spiritual, and sometimes physical). We have been warned. Many in this church had not participated in Satan's lies and Jesus assured them they would not be hurt by the present judgment or the future judgment that would come to man when Jesus ruled with a rod of iron. This was a warning and He urged them to hear with their spiritual ears. He promised to give them His own self when He promised they would receive the morning star.

03 REVELATION
Letter to the Churches II

Like all the other churches, the fifth letter written to Sardis was addressed to the shepherd, or pastor of the church. He signed it describing Himself as the One who has the sevenfold (denoting perfection) Holy Spirit (the Power Source) and the seven (denoting completion) stars (pastors). In other words, they are held by Him. He has the last say.

Jesus made it clear that He had unlimited knowledge (Omniscience) of their deeds. They had a reputation of being a great church, a really alive church, but we see He had nothing good to say about this church. He said they had a name as being alive, but they were really dead (spiritually). They were spiritually ineffective, or useless. Their spirituality was only a façade, as they solely went through the motions of being a great church. They probably had a beautiful building, marvelous music, a great youth and children's program, but programs have never replaced God's power. It is possible to talk the talk, go through the motions, but that doesn't fool Almighty God. They must not have been completely unconscious for Jesus warned them to wake up! They should focus on and strengthen what was left spiritually. Religious activity has never replaced Holy Spirit led spiritual worship and service.

Jesus wanted them to stir up what was left by remembering how it was when they first were saved. Most of us remember the zeal we had to truly serve the Lord at the beginning of our walk

11

with Him. They had a foundation, but it needed to be worked on. He warned them to watch for His Coming for He would come suddenly, unexpectedly, like a thief coming to rob. No second warning would come, so they needed to pay attention to what He was saying. The church was dying, but there were a few who hadn't given in to play-acting at church. There was a need to rise up and return fully to Him. To those who truly believed would be given white garment (declared sinless).

And their name would not be blotted out of the Book of Life. (This is not loss of salvation, only non-believers names would be blotted out of the Lamb's Book of Life.) God alone knows who the truly saved are. Many claim to be, but never truly accepted Him as their Savior and Lord. Also, some may look saved, but looks are deceiving.

Where this church received no commendation, the next, the Philadelphia Church, received no condemnation, for they had kept His Word. It was a gateway to other places; as they had to pass through this city when traveling to Lydia, Mysia, and Phrygia. Jesus described Himself as holy (set apart for God); true (no other truth apart from Jesus). He also stated that He held the key of David (the Messiah would come from line of David, Luke 2:4). No one could open a door He closed, or close one He opened. There are many liars, false prophets, who tried to stop the spread of Christianity. Some of them were even legalistic Jews who were religious leaders in the Jewish nation. We know today what Jesus claimed is true. And we see in this book that it will never happen no matter how powerful the non-believing world is. Truth will always reign.

Verse ten is a promise. Those of them, and we that persevere, will be kept from the horrible Tribulation that will come upon the world. It is God's nature to remove His own first, and then pass judgment. (Remember Noah and his family, Egypt and the Jews, Lot and Sodom and Gomorrah.) Not to say we won't see some pre-tribulation judgment before the Rapture, for we may.

Jesus admonished them to hold on to what they had. They had a crown promised (rewards) and a place reserved in the city of God, New Jerusalem. We also would have a new name and are citizens of His glory. He who has an ear, let him hear to what the (Holy) Spirit says to the church.

The church of Laodicea is thought by most Bible scholars and those who have read this book to be the Last Days Church. It is often called the "People's Church". Jesus signed this letter by calling Himself the Amen, (the last word) the faithful and true witness, the ruler of God's creation. He was simply re-iterating the truth that was written about Him already in the Word. (John 1:1-3, Hebrews 1:1-3, Revelation 22:12-13)

Laodicea was a wealthy city, a commercial and banking center. It had a famous garment industry and a medical school where they developed an eye ointment that they were famous for. A spirit of self-sufficiency had crept into this church. The Lord didn't have anything good to say about it. The Laodicean church represents the church today. It had knowledge but little wisdom, wealth but is poor spiritually, much humanism, secularism, and compromise. Jesus said it was lukewarm. He wished it was hot (on fire for Jesus) or cold (dead to the things of God). He said because it was neither, He would spit, or vomit, them out of His mouth. (Like coffee, good if it is very hot or iced, but lukewarm it gags one.)

They didn't need God or anyone else, they were so rich. They had fine clothes, but were really naked (needy) spiritually. He called them naked, poor, and blind (spiritually). He wanted them to anoint their spiritual eyes, put on spiritual clothing, and get gold from Him (spiritual riches). In other words, He wanted them to change their self-sufficiency into God-sufficiency. Not trust in earthly riches, but make spiritual riches their goal. Somewhere, they had become complacent to the Lord, and had become worldly. They went out into the world, and the world got into them. They lived just like the lost.

Jesus reminded them that those He loved, He chastened. Like a good Father, He would discipline them to turn them back to Him to repentance. He said He was knocking at the door (hearts door) pleading for them to let Him in. He wanted so much for them to return and fellowship with Him. A promise was given. If they would return to Him, they would share with His rule, just as Jesus sat on the throne given to Him by the Father.

This is the last time the church is ever mentioned in this book and most believe the Rapture takes place between chapters three and four, completing the Church Age. What follows is what we read in Daniel, the last seven weeks (years) designated to the Jews (not yet completed). It is not difficult to understand when you break the spiritual code, as I will attempt to do, so all can understand the last days before Jesus comes again.

04 REVELATION
John Taken To the Throne in Heaven

After having received the letters to the seven churches that were dictated to John from the risen Christ, John recorded them. John says in the fourth chapter, "After these things" referring to what had just occurred in chapters 1-3. (As I have mentioned before, most believe the Rapture took place between chapters 3-4, for the church is never mentioned again and it is God's character to take His children out of the world before He passes judgment.) He sees a door opened in heaven. Like a trumpet, loud and clear, he hears a voice speaking saying, "Come up here and I will show you things that must take place after this." These are events that will take place at the end, after the church age is over.

At once John was in the Spirit, he was given spiritual eyes to see the vision. What he saw was a glimpse of the throne of God, and God the Father sitting on that throne. He goes on and describes God's appearance as a jasper and sardius stone and there was a rainbow around the throne, which appeared like an emerald. Jasper stones, unlike today, were crystal clear and the sardius resembled a perfect ruby. These represent the awesome glory of God. Whenever we see a rainbow, it reminds us of God's promise to Noah to never destroy the world again with a flood.

This rainbow must have been beautiful, as it resembled an emerald. As spectacular as this was, John saw twenty-four elders seated on lesser thrones clothed in white robes with golden crowns on their heads. They represented the saved of all ages, twelve patriarchs, the foundation of the Law in the Old Testament, and the Church, the foundation of Grace in the New Testament. Their robes of white were signs of righteousness and the two groups represented the redeemed of all ages. Crowns of gold seem to show they had been judged already and were now with our Heavenly Father in Heaven.

The lightning, thunder, and voices from the throne we find refer to the unlimited power of the God sitting on the throne. Seven lamps burning before the throne again denotes the perfect Holy Spirit of God. Since the New Testament saints are found in heaven, it is understandable to see the Holy Spirit is no longer an indweller of the saints, but here in heaven with God. Before the throne was a sea of glass like crystal. If you have ever seen a crystal outside reflecting light, you can understand this sea reflected God's glory, as well as all directly before Him, a truly brilliant blinding light.

In the center and around the throne were four living creatures, covered with eyes in front and back. Like cherubim do, they guard God's throne. These creatures describe the attributes of God. Being full of eyes reflects his omniscience, His all knowing nature. The first creature was like a lion, representing God's omnipotence (unlimited power). The second was like a calf denoting meekness and faithful labor. The third had a face like a man describing Jesus' humanity and the fourth living creature was like a flying eagle, describing his majestic greatness. Some also think these living creatures represent all of creation, wild animals, tame animals, man, and fowl. These living creatures have six wings each, are full of eyes, and they do not rest day and night, symbolizing God's omnipresence (He is everywhere). All these represent all of creation worshipping God saying, "Holy, holy, holy, Lord God Almighty, Who was and is and it to come."

Whenever they do this, they give glory, honor, and thanks to Him who sits on the throne, who is eternal. The twenty-four elders fall down before Him also and worship, as well as cast their crowns before the throne saying, "You are worthy O Lord, To receive glory, honor and power; For You God, created all things and by Your will they exist and were created."

All of creation realizes only God, the Three In One, is worthy to receive praise, honor, and thanks. All creation finally realizes if there was anything good done in life, it was Him working through them. The crowns they received for their works on earth are cast at the Lord's throne, for only He deserves them. He is the Creator and Sustainer of the universe.

This glimpse of heaven was given to John to remind him, and us, of God's absolute control. God wanted John to be assured before the horrors, catastrophic events unfolded, that he could know beyond a shadow of a doubt God is in control, no matter what would occur.

05 REVELATION
The Search For One Worthy To Open Scroll

John sees God on the throne holding in His right hand a scroll written inside and on the back, sealed with seven seals. A strong angel was seen by John proclaiming with a loud voice, "Who is worthy to open the scroll and to loose its seals?" (Revelation 5:2) (The more seals, the more important the document.) Roman wills were sealed with seven seals. Only an authorized person could open the seals. John knew it was an important scroll and included an important message. No one in heaven or on the earth or under the earth was able to open the scroll, or look at it. So John wept.

But one of the elders said to John, "Do not weep. Behold, the Lion of the tribe of Judah, (Genesis 49:9-10) the Root of David, (King David was from the tribe of Judah, and the Messiah had been predicted to come out of that tribe, Shiloh was another name used to denote Jesus, Who would have an everlasting kingdom. (I Chronicles 17:11-12) He has prevailed to open the scroll and to loose its seven seals." This referred to His two roles, at the First Coming the Suffering Servant, the Perfect Sacrifice for Sin. At the Second Coming, He will come in supremacy, the King of Kings and the Lord of Lords to judge all men. This was a part of the code unveiled in what was already spoken in the Old Testament Word.

In the midst of the throne, in the midst of the elders, stood a Lamb as though it had been slain, having seven horns and seven eyes, which are the seven Spirits of God. When John the Baptist saw Jesus coming he said, "Behold! The Lamb of God who takes away the sin of the world!" (John 1:29) This was John's testimony to who Jesus was and what He had come to do. He was the sacrificial Lamb to pay the price for sin for all of us... forever. He was worthy to open the seals. He has earned that authority at Calvary. This symbolic description tells us that Jesus alone is worthy. Here He had seven horns, describing His unlimited power, seven eyes, denoting His unlimited wisdom and knowledge, and He had the complete Holy Spirit. All eyes were focused on Jesus. He then came and took the scroll from God who sat on the throne.

When Jacob prophesied of his twelve sons future, he said the scepter or rule would not depart from Judah until Shiloh, (the Messiah, Jesus) would come. (Genesis 49:10) Jesus was the Root of David from the tribe of Judah. David was promised his kingdom would never end. (I Chronicles 17:11-12) Jesus fulfilled that prophecy, being the direct descendant of King David. (Matthew 1:5-6) This fulfilled the prophecy that Jesus would come at His first Coming as a Suffering Servant, and the suffering sacrificial lamb for payment of our sins once and for all. (Hebrews 9:28)

He would also be a King of Kings and Lord of Lords and come in power and supremacy at the Second Coming. The roles were not contradictory, though the Jews ignored His meekness at the First Coming to die for our sins. This had been foretold all along, but they didn't want a servant, they wanted a king. He would come to the earth as king, but not until His Second Coming to rule during the thousand-year reign (Millennium).

When John saw standing in the midst of the throne a Lamb as though it had been slain, having seven horns and seven eyes, he knew exactly who it was. John the Baptist had called Jesus "the Lamb of God which takes away the sin of the world." (John 1:29) John knew Jesus was worthy to open the seals. Only Jesus fulfilled this description. The seven horns describe Jesus' unlimited power and His seven eyes describe His unlimited knowledge. The number seven also denoted the complete Holy Spirit sent out to the whole world.

When He took the scroll out of God's hand all creation, all the saved from the Old and New Testament, with harps and golden bowls of incense (incense represented the prayers of the saints), sang a new song. They sang Jesus is worthy to open the seals for He had died and redeemed all to God from every nation and He has made us kings and priests to our God. We will reign with Him on earth. (Revelation 5:9-10) Whereas as in the last chapter all of creation had worshipped God, now countless numbers of angels around the throne worship and sang praising Jesus Christ attributing power, honor, and glory to Him. Then, all praised Father and Son saying, "Blessing and honor and glory and power be to Him who sits on the throne, and to the Lamb, forever and ever."

The message of this chapter was that we should not fear judgment. God is in control. We will reign with Jesus. All of creation will praise Him for who He is and what He has done. Jesus paid the price in full and because of that, we understand about God's love and that of His Son Jesus. We have nothing to fear, especially not the judgments about to be revealed.

06 REVELATION
The Six Seal Judgments

After seeing and being assured of God's absolute rule and control of the world and all creation, John was then allowed to begin to see the coming judgments that would unfold in the end times. John knew God and His Son were worthy, and sufficient to receive all power and glory. They alone were deserving of this. Now John was prepared to receive the full revelation of what was in store in the future. Jesus the only worthy One begins by opening the First Seal of the scroll, which ushers in the Seven Seal Judgments.

Much has been written and spoken on T.V., movies, and even in our pulpits about the four horses of the Apocalypse. In fact Christians and non-Christians are very familiar with them, but know nothing of the truth of them. Many believe they are mere fantasy, which is absolutely untrue. When the Lamb (Jesus) opened the First of the seven seals, John heard a thunderous voice of one of the living creatures bidding him to "Come and see." A white horse appeared with one sitting on it carrying a bow with a crown on his head, and told to go out and conquer. Satan (the head of the counterfeit Trinity) wanted to fool the world into believing he, (not God) was in charge of the world, along with the Anti-Christ, not the true Christ, the Son of God, but the counterfeit Christ, and we will later see the False Prophet is Satan's counterfeit Holy Spirit, rather in reality, he is the un-holy Spirit.

The crown symbolized a ruler. Notice in his hand was a bow, but he didn't carry any arrows. In other words, his intent was to rule the world. Though he came on a white horse as a conqueror, his weapon was to deceive and offer what the world had longed for so many years, peace. (Matthew 24:24) He would deceive even Israel without warfare. We today, as a world, are ripe for this, as the world is tired of war and terrorism. The land of Israel is more susceptible than any other, due to the constant threat of war. The book of Daniel states a leader will come who will make a covenant of peace with Israel. (Daniel 9:27) The Anti-Christ will soon exchange the bow for a sword. (I Thessalonians 5:3-5) The First Seal reveals that the Anti-Christ coming into the world will be the first of the judgments.

The Second Seal was opened and John again was told to "Come and see." There appeared another horse, fiery red, and the rider was granted to take peace from the earth. He was given a great sword and men would kill one another. This represents world war. Red often refers to terror and violence. This is the "Beast" (Anti-Christ) which foretells what type of world dictator the Anti-Christ will truly be.

The Third Seal was opened and John beheld a rider on a black horse with a pair of scales in his hand. A voice was heard from the third living creature saying, "a quart of wheat for a denarius, (a day's wage in that time) and three quarts of barley for a denarius, but do not harm the oil and the wine. (Luxury items in that day) (Revelation 6:6) This speaks of world famine. Famine and war go together. A food shortage drives up prices and forces government rationing. Many farmers are selling good farm land today, and it will take a man a full day's wages to feed his family during this time. Many countries do this today due to war and famine. There will be plenty of luxury items for those who sell out to the Anti-Christ.

When the Fourth Seal was opened accompanied by the voice from the fourth living creature he again told John to "Come and see." A pale horse and a rider appeared called "Death and Hades." Power was given to kill with the sword 1/4th of the earth with hunger and death and by the Beast of the earth. (Revelation 6:7-8) This represents 1/4th of the earth being killed by war, famine, plague, and wild beasts. In war it is impossible to be clean and organized. Many new super viruses are now popping up everywhere, so no telling how bad the pestilences will be. For a fraction of the cost of an A-bomb, bacteriological bombs, could wipe of all of California. When beasts have no food, they will eat humans. This is a terrible picture of devastation. But, remember, we Christians (Church) will have all have been taken to Heaven before these judgments are passed and we will be forever with Christ. These judgments will be for those who have rejected His loving call. This should give us an urgency to share the good news that Jesus loves all men and doesn't want even one of them to endure these judgments. (2 Peter 3:9)

The Fifth Seal is opened and world persecution for faith occurs. John saw under the altar the souls slain for their faith in the Word and their testimony. They cried out to God with a loud voice, "How long, O Lord," the cry of God's people throughout the ages for justice on those who persecuted them. Each was given a white robe showing they had been redeemed by the blood and were finally receiving the vengeance they had sought. It is clear, and we will see in our next chapter, that some lost people will be saved during the Great Tribulation, but many of them will be martyred.

In verse 15 we see when the Sixth Seal is opened there was a great earthquake and the sun became blackened and the moon became like blood. The stars of heaven fell to the earth like a fig tree dropped its figs when shaken by a mighty wind. This was no ordinary earthquake. It will put to shame the worse we have ever had before and it will not just affect a region of the world, but the entire world. The phenomena of the moon as blood has already been seen in certain areas like Los Angeles due to heavy fog. I have myself seen this caused by the smoke of wild fires.

The stars falling to earth could be missiles or meteors, or it could just be occurring due to God's wrath or by natural or nuclear phenomena. In verses 14-17, we see the sky like a scroll rolling up on its self. This describes a nuclear explosion whereby the atmosphere rolls back on itself. This could be, but it matters not what caused it, natural or nuclear. Every mountain and island will be moved out of its place. This describes a great cosmic upheaval, and it is catastrophic. Men will cry out for the rocks and mountains to fall on them. For God's great day and His wrath have come and at that time, who can stand? I know I will not endure this, I wish I could be sure none of my dearly loved family or friends won't either. The time to repent is NOW!

07 REVELATION
The Sealing of 144,000 Jews

Six of the seven Seals of Judgment have been opened. The White Horse - The Anti-Christ, symbolizing a beastly dictator will come on the scene. The Red Horse – symbolizing war and bloodshed will take place. The Black Horse symbolizing famine. It will take a day's wages to feed a family. The Pale Horse symbolizing mass death and epidemics, the natural result of war and famine. Great martyrdom then takes place when the Fifth Seal is opened. And the sixth seal, a great earthquake, such as never seen before, that was so powerful every mountain and island was moved. Before the seventh Seal is opened, God is seen sealing His own nation Israel.

The first thing that John sees after this is four angels standing at the four corners of the earth, holding the four winds, the North, East, South and West so that they should not blow on the land, sea or trees. Another angel came from the east and had the seal of the living God and was told "Do not harm the earth or sea, or the trees till we have sealed the servants of our God on their foreheads." The numbers to be sealed were 144,000 of all the tribes of the children of Israel, 12,000 from each tribe. These were not Mormons, Jehovah Witnesses or any other, solely Jews. Though all genealogical records are lost, God knows each and where they are. We know that a seal denotes ownership. Later Satan will seal his own with the number 666. (Revelation 13:16-18) Today God's people are sealed with the Holy Spirit. (Ephesians 1:13-14) The moment they are saved, this seal is our guarantee that we belong and are safe in Him. The 144,000 Jews will receive the Father's Name on their foreheads as their seal. (Revelation 14:1) God's seal will protect God's chosen Jews from the judgments that will hurt the earth, land, and sea when the four angels blow their trumpets.

The tribe of Levi is included though given no inheritance. Dan and Ephraim were the first tribes to lead the Jews into idolatry and are not included. God has promised to never abandon His chosen people no matter how badly they have treated Him. (Romans 11:1, 25-27) When the last Gentile is saved during the church age, God will give the Jews their last seven years allotted to them. (The last week spoke by Daniel, seven years.) This will complete the seventy weeks (490 years) allotted to them.

In Verse 9 John sees a numberless multitude of Gentiles from all nations, tribes, people, and tongues standing before the throne. What a revival! They wore white robes, and stood before Christ (the Lamb) with palm branches in their hands (Victors). They were praising God and the Lamb with loud voices saying, "Salvation belongs to our God who sits on the throne, and to the Lamb." (Revelation 7:10) Also around the throne were angels, elders, and the four living creatures (representing all of creation) worshipping, praising, and giving thanks to our God forever and ever. Amen.

One of the elders asked John who these were in white robes, and where did they come from? John said, "Sir, you know." In other words, you surely know, I don't. What follows answers the question asked and debated through the years. The angel told John these were those saved during the tribulation. Yes, there will be some saved, but it will not be easy. If they refuse to take the mark of the Beast, they will not be able to buy or sell even the barest of necessities. They refused to take Satan's mark, suffered much, and even some were martyred. Now they wore white robes (denotes righteousness) and made them white in the blood of the Lamb. They were standing in front of the throne with all the others and will dwell forever with God and He will see they are never hungry or thirsty. Heat or nothing else will harm them. And God will wipe away every tear from their eyes. (Never any more sadness.)

08 REVELATION
The Seventh Seal Ushers In the Seven Trumpet Judgments

We have seen the nation of Israel will turn from its unbelief to faith and God will seal 144,000 Jews from every tribe with a seal on their foreheads denoting His possession and protection. Also we saw a great multitude from every nation, tribe peoples and tongues, before the throne in white robes. John was told these were victors saved through the tribulation and God Himself would protect them from hunger, thirst, and heat. God would wipe away every tear from their eyes. This answers the question, "Will any Gentiles be saved during the Tribulation?"

The Seventh Seal was opened and an interlude of ½ of an hour of silence occurred. It was like the anticipation of a foreman of a jury waiting for the verdict of said jury. This is like the lull before a storm or an eye of a hurricane. This Seventh seal issued in the First Trumpet Judgment. John saw seven angels who were given seven trumpets. Another angel had a golden censer given with much incense to offer with the prayers of the saints on the golden altar before the throne. The smoke of the incense, together with the prayers of the saints went up before God from the angel's hand.

The angel took the censer and filled it with fire from the altar and hurled it to the earth. There came peals of thunder, rumblings, flashes of lightnings, and an earthquake. This was not to harm the earth. This was the beginning of an ecological nightmare. This was not to harm man, but to warn of the judgment to come. Four would harm the earth and three would be aimed at man himself. Then, the angels prepared to sound their trumpets.

The First Trumpet sounded and there came hail and fire mixed with blood, and it was hurled upon the earth. The result was 1/3 of the earth's trees burned up and all green grass was burned up. (Remember ¼ of the earth and its people have already been destroyed.) This would include fruit trees, wheat, oats, rye, and other grasses. Not only would this be disastrous, but when we add erosion of the soil, we see just how this would affect the world's food supply.

When the Second Trumpet sounded and something like a huge mountain ablaze was thrown into the sea, 1/3 of the sea was turned to blood and 1/3 of the living sea creatures died, as well as 1/3 of the merchant vessels were destroyed. (The sea covers ¾ of the earth.) Many people depend upon fish for their diet around the world. (This reminds us of the plague against Egypt in Exodus 7:17-18) The U.S.A. depends upon the merchant vessels to carry food and other products to and from the nations of the world.

Our attention goes to the third angel who sounds the Third Trumpet. A blazing star falls and hits all the rivers and springs of fresh water of the earth. This star was called Wormwood. In other words, it turned the fresh water to bitter, undrinkable water. Included in this would be the Amazon River, the longest river in the world at 4,000 miles long and the Mississippi River 3,710 miles long. There are only one hundred principal rivers in the world, and 1/3 of them were struck. When you add all the wells and other fresh water springs that have been made useless, this is a terrible judgment. Many different people will die due to this.

The fourth angel sounded the Fourth Trumpet and 1/3 of the sun, moon, and stars were struck rendering them dark. (This was parallel to the ninth plague of Egypt.) One-third of daylight was darkened. This would cause vast changes in the temperatures of the earth. No telling how many people will be depending upon solar energy at this time. One-third of the day and night will be darkened. As John watched, an eagle flew in mid-air and called out in a loud voice, "Woe! Woe! Woe to the inhabitants of the earth." Because of what had already happened due to the trumpet blasts.

There were still three more and they would intensify, and the severity would be greater. God was leaving 2/3 light because of His mercy. He was giving man a chance to repent and turn to Him.

The first four Trumpet Judgments were directed toward the world's ecology. The last three will be directed toward man himself.

09 REVELATION
Two Judgments, Locusts, Four Demons, and 200 Million Troops

John hears the fifth angel sound the Fifth Trumpet, and sees a star fall from the sky. This is no ordinary star that we see in the sky at night, nor is it a star like our movie, T.V., or athletic stars. This star is a person and we get a clue to his identity when we are told he is given a key to the Abyss, a home of demons. (Luke 8:31) Since Revelation 9:11 says the angel in charge of the Abyss is the Destroyer, Satan himself, we have a confirmation. We also see later that Satan and his fallen angels are confined under lock and key; confined there during the thousand year reign on earth of Jesus Christ. (Revelation 20:1-3)

When Satan used the key and opened the Abyss, smoke like a giant furnace came out and darkened the sun and sky. John says he saw locusts come down to earth and given power like scorpions to cause severe pain. They had a painful sting and were told not to harm any vegetation, but rather people who did not have the seal of God on their foreheads. Though the sting by these demons was so horrendous many would cry out for death to overtake them, they were not given the power to kill, just to torture people for five months. Normally, locusts destroy all vegetation and can be so bad they bring drought and famine. But these are no ordinary locusts.

Roman soldiers, who would not even flinch under normal pain, would scream out in pain when bit by these scorpions (Normal scorpions).

John describes these locusts, but we have to remember he was using familiarities of his day. One can imagine if in the 1920s we tried to describe a jet, a computer, a smart phone, or a fully loaded modern day car or a drone. John's description was that these locusts looked like horses prepared for battle, awesome. Human faces having crowns of gold, woman's hair like a robot of today. They had lion's teeth, beastly, savage and having iron-like breastplates (Hard to kill). They had wings and sounded like horse drawn chariots rushing into battle. (Many of our vets came home and told how when they looked over the mountain and saw a large group of helicopters coming they sounded and looked like a mass of locusts.) Many of our present day armaments have the ability to harm like these did and their tails carry their sting. Now, whether these are literal or symbolic we cannot be sure, but either way, I'm glad I won't be around. Many of our young people are being desensitized of horror by T.V., video games, movies, and books. They will not be as awestruck as John was in his day. In verse eleven, John says they had a king over them named Abaddon or Apollyon (Translated Destroyer). Satan himself led this onslaught. In verse twelve, we see one woe is past, but there are two to come. (Webster defines a woe as a condition of deep suffering, affliction or grief, or a calamity.)

The sixth angel sounds his Sixth Trumpet and a voice is heard from the horns (symbolic of power) from the golden altar that is before God. The sixth angel was instructed to release the four demonic angels (so horrendous they had been under lock and key, kept there by God under the great Euphrates River). They had been kept there for this very hour and were released to kill 1/3 of mankind. They led 200 million mounted troops for battle. On May 21, 1995, China boasted in Time magazine of having such a mounted Calvary. The colors were fiery red, dark blue, and yellow as sulfur, colors China uses nationally. The result is 1/3 of mankind is killed by the three plagues of fire, smoke, and sulfur, which came out of their mouths and their tails.

The rest of mankind still did not repent of the work of their hands. They didn't cease their worship of demons, idols, gold, silver, bronze, or stone. Nor did they cease and repent of their murders, magical arts, sexual immorality, or their theft. It is hard to foresee man becoming so evil, but remember, God has already many in heaven with him. And also remember the Convictor, the Holy Spirit, has been taken out of the world. Man left to his own evil delusions and devices is an animal, worse than an animal.

10 REVELATION
The Angel and the Little Scroll

Revelation Chapter 10-14 describes events that take place around the middle of the Tribulation, the book we are trying to familiarize ourselves with. The Anti-Christ began to make his conquest by promising peace, and protecting Israel. After 3 ½ years he will break his agreement, invade the temple, and begin to persecute those Jews he promised to protect.

John saw a mighty angel coming down from heaven in a cloud. In the Old Testament whenever "The Angel of the Lord" was mentioned, it was an Old Testament appearance, or epiphany, of Jesus Christ. If Scripture denoted an angel of the Lord, it was an ordinary angel of the Lord. (Exodus 3:2, Judges 2:4, 6:11-13, and verses 21-22 are a few of the appearances of "The Angel of the Lord". As we see this angel described, we see it is most likely the mighty King Jesus. In the Old Testament a cloud represented the glory of God. The Israelites were led by day with a cloud (God's Presence). When Moses met God in the temple, a cloud was over the temple. A cloud was on Mt. Sinai when Moses went up and met with God. We see in Revelation 4:3 Jesus is described as having a rainbow around his head. In Revelation 5:5, He is called a Lion from the tribe of Judah, referring to His wrathful judgment. So since He roars like a lion, we see this angel is none other than Jesus. His face was as the sun and His feet like pillars of fire, another way of describing God's Only Begotten Son, Jesus. (Signs of judgment, which He was passing with more severity.)

The Anti-Christ will soon become the savage dictator he has been deceiving the whole world about. The world will be under his control, but before this happens, the Savior stands with His right foot on the sea, His left foot on the land, and claims the whole world as His possession. He cries with a loud voice and claims the land and sea for Himself. This was the inheritance that His Father promised Him. (Psalm 2:6-9)

When He cried out seven thunders uttered their voices, but John was told to seal these things up and not to write them down, whereas before John had been told to write all that He saw. It is useless to speculate why he was told to seal only this. The Angel of God raised His hand to heaven and swears by Him who lives forever and ever, who created the heaven and the things in it, and the sea and everything in it, that there should not be any more delay in sounding the Seventh Trumpet. (Seen in chapter 11.)

John was told to take the little scroll (or book) which is in the open hand of the angel who stands on the sea and on the land. John did what was told to him, "Take and eat it; and it will make your stomach bitter, but it will be as sweet as honey in your mouth." John obeyed and when he ate it, it was as sweet as honey in his mouth. But when he had eaten it, his stomach became bitter. The Word is like that to some people. They love to hear it, study it, sing about it, but they feel it is a bitter pill to swallow. It is hard to obey those areas that touch on their sin. John was told afterwards he must prophesy again to many peoples, nations, tongues, and kings. Surely, as we read his record of this book, he is still speaking today.

11 REVELATION
The Two Witnesses

This is the center of the book of Revelation. The last 3 ½ years from here on out are often called the Great Tribulation. An angel gives the apostle John a reed like a measuring rod and tells him to

"Rise and measure the temple of God, the altar, and those who worship there." (All belonged to Him.) But he was told to omit the outer court outside the temple, for it was given to the Gentiles. They would trample the holy city underfoot for forty-two months (3 ½ years). The only person who has the right to measure land is the owner. The temple belonged to God. The Jews, who have been deceived by the Anti-Christ, were now receiving who He was through revelation. He and the Gentiles had taken temporary control not only of the temple, but the holy city of Jerusalem. Now, He has revealed himself for who and what He is, proclaiming Himself as being God.

It was revealed to John that He would give power to two witnesses and they will prophesy for the latter 1,260 days (42 months, or 3 ½ years of Great Tribulation). They would be clothed in sackcloth (symbolic of mourning, or heavy affliction). He called them two olive trees, and two lamp stands standing before God. Oil came from olive trees, and lamps were often filled with oil for power. (Both are symbolic that the prophesiers would be filled with the Holy Spirit; often oil was symbolic of Holy Spirit in the Word.) Thus, they would be powerful men filled with the Holy Spirit. Much speculation has gone into who these two were. Some interpret them as Elijah and Moses, because of mention of powerful miracles worked through them. Others say Elijah and Enoch, as they never died; they were just taken to heaven by the Lord. (Some claim they were but a type of these men.)

Whoever they were, they were empowered by God Himself and mightily used. These witnesses will be a threat to the evil world for 3 ½ years, as no one could harm them. Fire proceeded from their mouth and they could and did devour their enemies. They had power to keep rain from falling, could turn the waters to blood, and strike the earth with plagues as often as they desired. Surely, one of their messages preached was that salvation came from accepting the blood of Jesus Christ as the only way to have eternal life. Also their messages preached the need of repentance of evil and acceptance of the only righteousness as found in Jesus alone. When their testimony was finished, the Anti-Christ will ascend out of the bottomless pit, make war against them, and kill them. (Where he comes from reveals who he is.)

The bodies of these godly men will lie in the streets of the Holy City for 3 ½ days. Here it is called Sodom and Egypt as well as it was where Jesus was crucified at Calvary. (Evil was done here.) A great time of merriment takes place. People will celebrate and make merry, because their preaching will no longer convict and torment them. They will actually send gifts to one another for at last, those preachers are gone. They will gloat, and will be watched on T.V. around the world. (Years ago, no one understood how this could happen, as there were no T.Vs. or other electronic aids.) They will refuse to let anyone bury these witnesses, so the rejoicing would continue. But wait, after 3 ½ days, they will be raised from the dead. Celebration would be replaced by great fear by all who see this. They heard a loud voice say, "Come up here." As their enemies watched, they ascended to heaven in a cloud.

In the same hour, there was a great earthquake and 1/10th of the city fell. Seven thousand people were killed. The rest were filled with fear and gave glory to the God of heaven. This was the second woe, and the third woe was coming quickly. The seventh angel sounded and voices were heard in heaven saying, "The kingdoms of this world have become the kingdoms of our Lord and of His Christ, and He shall reign forever and ever!" (Revelation 11:15-16) The twenty four elders, (representing all Israel and the Church of Jesus Christ), fell on their faces and gave thanks, praise, and worshipped the Lord God Almighty. He has finally taken reign and passed judgment, vindicating His people. He would give rewards to all small and great who feared His name and He would destroy those who destroyed the earth.

The temple of God was opened and the ark of His covenant (representing His Presence) was seen, accompanied by lightnings, noises, thunderings, an earthquake, and great hail. This reminded all of His power.

12 REVELATION
The Pregnant Woman and The Dragon

One of the basic beliefs of Christians is in the Holy Trinity; God is three in one… Father, Son, and the Holy Spirit. It is hard to completely understand, but by faith in God's own Word, we believe though a mystery, it is truth. They are equal in worth and power, but their functions are different. In the Old Testament, we mainly see God the Father at work. We know in John 3:16 that God so loved us that He sent His only begotten Son to pay the payment once and for all for sin. In order to receive that gift, we must ask Jesus to forgive us of all our sins, past, present, and future, and believe He came into the world to save us by offering Himself as payment for those sins at Calvary. When Jesus resurrected to go back to be with the Father in heaven, He told us He was going away, but His Holy Spirit would then come and be in us as Indweller. (John 14:16-18) Jesus took the center stage in the New Testament, and we see the Holy Spirit took center stage in the early church. So since then, He has been in and works through each and every Believer. (John 16:7-8, 17)

What so many do not know is that Satan has an unholy Trinity. He has counterfeited everything that God stands for and is the arch enemy of our Lord. He tries to imitate God, has tried to take His throne, and counterfeits all three personages, including the Holy Spirit. In Isaiah 14:13-15 we see Lucifer, previously a beautiful angel, was cast out of heaven and was cast down to earth for that sin. Lucifer is none other than Satan. Satan thought by getting rid of Jesus Christ at Calvary, He would get rid of his problem. But the only thing is He was used of God the Father to work out salvation for all who believe with their hearts. We will be introduced to the unholy Spirit, the false prophet in this record of the end times, as he promotes the Anti-Christ as the true Messiah. The main task of the Holy Spirit is to point men to Christ, by convicting them of their sins, and guiding them to all truth. As Jesus was God Himself, Satan will indwell the Anti-Christ in the latter days. He is the author of all evil. I thought this would be helpful to understand before we meet Satan's counterfeit personalities and deception.

Though we saw the seventh trumpet was sounded in chapter 11, we will see the details in chapter 16. As we see chapter 12 unfold, we see that God's and Satan's acts increase in frequency and intensity. The first thing we see is that a sign appears in heaven. A woman clothed with the sun, the moon, and on her head a garland of twelve stars. Then being with child, she cried out in labor and gives birth to a man child. This woman is none other than Israel. In Genesis 37:9-10, we see in Joseph's dream he shared with his brothers and father Jacob that the sun was his father and the moon his mother. The twelve stars on the woman seen were represented of Jacob's twelve sons. (Twelve tribes and descendants who would inherit the promises of the nation Israel.) The child was symbolic of the Messiah, Jesus who would be born directly from Jacob's lineage. (Genesis 49:1, 22-26)

Another sign appeared in heaven. A fiery red dragon having seven heads, ten horns, and seven crowns on his head. This huge dragon was Satan himself. The ten horns represent ten countries which are the nucleus of the beast's empire (Anti-Christ's). Most believe it will be the renewal of the former Roman Empire. The seven heads and seven crowns represent the seven principal powerful leaders of the countries. The dragon's tail sweeps 1/3 of stars to earth. (Probably referring back to when Satan and his demonic angels were cast out of heaven for their rebellion against God.) (Isaiah 14:12-15) He waits to devour Israel's child as soon as he was born. Jesus is that Messiah. Herod tried to do this, but an angel warned them and they fled to Egypt till Herod was dead. Though Herod had all the male children less than two- years-old destroyed, he failed. At Jesus' First Coming, He was a tender root, a suffering servant, but He will rule the nations with a rod of iron, as prophesied in Psalm 2:9. In verse 5 of Revelation 12, the child being snatched up to heaven refers to the ascension of Jesus after the crucifixion.

The woman (Israel) fled to the desert to the place prepared for her to be cared for by God for 1,260 days, 42 months, or 3 ½ years, the time of the last half of the Great Tribulation. One of the great wonders of the world is the history of the Jewish nation Israel. The world over and over has tried to annihilate the Jews. Yet despite the special hatred of Satan, and the evil people he fills with Anti-Semitism, they have failed. Think of Pharaoh, Hamaan in the book of Esther, Nebuchadnezzar when Jews were carried off in exile to Babylon, and Hitler during the Holocaust, all these energized by Satan failed miserably. Muslims today have plans to destroy the Jews and make it known to the whole world. They don't know our God like I do. His love and plans for them have never changed. (Romans 11:25-27) Is it any wonder that God Himself will hide the Jews during the last 3½ years of the Great Tribulation. Many believe it will be in Petra. It matters not where this is, when Jesus protects you, you have nothing to fear.

War breaks out in heaven between Satan and the saints of God. Apparently Satan makes one last try at usurping God from His throne, to no avail. This time he and his demons are defeated by Michael and his angels. Never again will they be allowed to go back to heaven. This time it is permanent. No more will he be able to go before the throne and slander God's children. Day and night, he has gone before God's throne to do this. No more! At last, the prayers of the saints have been answered. Jesus secured their salvation by the blood of the Lamb and they did not love their lives more than death. But woe to the inhabitants of the earth, for Satan has come down to you. Because he knows his time is short, he will do all he can to harm all people of the earth and to drown out their testimony.

Many have tried to see where the U.S.A. is in all this. Here in verses 12:13-15 is a passage which says Satan makes another onslaught on the Jews, but the woman (Jews) was given two wings of a great eagle that she might fly into the wilderness to her place where she will have the safety she has been promised by God. Since the eagle is our national bird, many believe we will provide a great airlift for the Jews to a place of safety. It matters not who or what happens, she will be in the safety of the Lord's delivering power. Pursuing the woman, Satan originates a flood. Whether real or just a metaphor slandering words, we do not know; it just could be a final onslaught on God's people. The Bible clearly states the earth opened its mouth and swallowed up the flood. No doubt, Satan continued to annihilate God's people.

13 REVELATION

The Powerful Beast

In this chapter, the focus is on the coming world government and the Beast, (Anti-Christ) and the False Prophet who is the counterfeit Holy Spirit. We will also see that they are energized by Satan himself (the Dragon).

What we need to realize is there has been throughout history many who are anti Christ (those who are against Christ and all He stands for). But this Anti-Christ will come in the middle of the Tribulation and reveal his true identity. He is a real person and up till now, he has been a deceiver. He is the rider on the white horse with bow, but no arrows found in Revelation 6:2. Now 3 ½ years later, he is revealing his true identity.

John is standing on the sand of the sea and is given another vision. He sees rising out of that sea, (the sea refers to the masses of Gentile peoples) (Isaiah 57:20, Rev. 17:15) a beast having seven heads and ten horns with ten crowns on them. This refers to his nature, a cruel beastly individual. The ten heads refers to ten countries and the horns with crowns tell us that they are leaders who are very powerful. Europe has long wanted a United Europe much like the U.S.A. The European Market was the beginning. It started with eight nations, and now has twenty-five. This has varied at times, and will continue. We saw the exit of Great Britain (BREXIT), as they realized they were no longer in control of their own country's decisions. We saw a new world thought, a new ideal. The words geo-political and talk of a common financial system became more to be desired by some. This would place all nations under a world-wide government and this is just the beginning of a catastrophe. Can you imagine having the same say as countries like Sudan, and Bangladesh? The blasphemous name on his heads shows us the world-wide government will be everything that Satan desires, not our God's Will, Way, and Word.

Further description shows us that the Anti-Christ will be much like former empires, tyrannical. He uses the example of three former empires as an example: a leopard, a bear and a lion. He will be eloquent, arrogant, savage, and a world conqueror like Alexander the Great. John is told that the Anti-Christ is energized by Satan who gives him his great power and authority to reign. We see that the Anti-Christ "seemed" to receive a mortal wound and that wound was healed. There has been much discussion about this. Some think it was the former Roman Empire that died. However, the verses that follow, point to it being the Anti-Christ with his great deceptive nature himself that receives the mortal wound. He performs the greatest hoax of all times. He may have lived through an actual assassination attempt that would've caused this. And his resurrection was staged. After all, he wants to imitate Christ and His resurrection.

In the days we now live in, we are already seeing how easy it is to lead people to believe a lie. It is called "Perception Management". You tell people what they want to hear over and over. After a while, they believe what they heard, because it is what they want. The word "seemed" is a glimpse into the truth. In verse four, we see the results as men worshipped the Dragon (Satan) and the Beast (the Anti-Christ). They were convinced no one could be as mighty as the Beast, after all, no one can raise the dead. If you know the Bible like I do, men can perform black magic to an extent, but even Satan cannot bring anyone back to life again, only our Almighty God. This man was given this power for only forty-two months, a temporary ability for God's purpose.

After he blasphemed God's name, he was given power to blaspheme God's holy tabernacle. The result will be that all the lost men from around the world will follow him, anyone whose names were not written in the Book of Life. This is perplexing what God inserts here, no matter what happens, you have an ear so listen. No matter what happens, you remain in whatever state you are in, even in suffering, captivity, and even to the death. God is still in control. He will level the grounds, in His perfect time.

John sees another beast coming out of the earth. He had only two horns (limited power) like a lamb, but spoke like a dragon (like the devil). Where the Anti-Christ was a world-wide political leader, this person is a world-wide religious leader. His main task is to counterfeit the Holy Spirit and to point men to worship and follow the Anti-Christ (He is an unholy spirit). He will be given great authority and he will perform great signs (miracles). He will even be able to call down fire from heaven in the sight of men like Elijah did in I Kings 18:38. He is such a great deceiver, being granted to perform signs, that he deceives the lost world by making an image of the Beast that speaks and has breath. He causes many to worship this image or be killed. (II Thessalonians 2:3-4, Matthew 24:23-25)

We don't need to think how easy it would be to do this with the electronic knowledge we already have. This could even be done today with our technology. Microchips are becoming smaller and smaller doing more than ever before. We don't even have to be nearby to operate such a mechanism. All we need is a remote T.V., a great teeny microphone, a robot, and a remote to operate the image from a distance. Even some cars today can be operated without a driver. Man is so primed to believe a lie.

The mark 666 is finally revealed. Most have already heard of this mark of the Beast and try to convince people that it has to be our Social Security Number, our Credit Card, or some other government I.D. It could be as simple an explanation as since the number seven is perfection, the number six would denote a less than perfect individual, but high among created species, thus 666 could just be the number of man. In the New Testament, we see all saints have the Indwelling Holy Spirit in them to prove we belong to Christ. It is our guarantee that we are His. (Ephesians 1:13) Here we see the Anti-Christ is doing another thing god-like, so he requires all people to receive his mark of 666 on their right hand or forehead. Without this mark, a person cannot sell or buy at all. Makes you wonder how the Israelites made it wandering in the desert without any food or drink for forty years. Oh, that's right, Manna and water from a rock!

14 REVELATION
The Lamb and the 144,000

This chapter is parenthetical (like inside parentheses), in other words, it is a glimpse of up-coming events. It is just like our Lord to show His people the end results before they happen. It takes the edge off the judgment to soon follow. John looks and sees Jesus (the Lamb) standing in Mount Zion, and standing with Him in heaven were the 144,000 Jews with the Father's name written on their foreheads. (They belonged to Him and this was their ultimate destination.) John heard the powerful voice of God like many waters and the voice of a loud peal of thunder. Though powerful, the voice was pleasant sounding like harpists playing their harps. They sang a new song before the throne, before all creation, (four living creatures) and the twenty-four elders (representing all O.T. and N.T. saints). No one could understand the song, but the 144,000 Jews who had been redeemed from the earth. There were those who were not defiled with women and who were virgins. (They had not committed spiritual adultery and many had never married, their true love was the Lord.)

They followed the Lamb (Jesus Christ) wherever He went. They were the pure, purchased, redeemed of God and the first fruits to God and the Lamb. They were considered faultless, perfect at last, before the throne of God. John saw another angel flying in mid-air having the eternal gospel to preach to all men no matter what race, citizenship, language, or people. He cried out with a loud voice, "Fear God and give Him the glory because the hour of His judgment has come. Worship Him who made the heavens, the earth, the sea and the springs of water. (Not the Anti-Christ) Revelation 14:7 NIV

A second angel follows and cries, "Babylon (the evil, corrupt world system led by the Anti Christ) is fallen, is fallen, that great city because she has made all nations drink of the wine of the wrath of her fornication (Spiritual adulteries, with the help of the false prophet). Evidence seems to point to Babylon on the Euphrates River being re-built and the capital of the world. Although many scholars believe Rome, Italy will be. We will discuss this later in chapter 18.

A warning is given by the third angel to those still deciding whether to follow the Beast (Anti-Christ, world leader) or not. Count the cost! The easy way has always been the wrong way. If anyone worships the Beast and his image and receives his mark on his forehead or hand, he, too, will drink of the wine of God's fury, which has been poured full strength (not watered down) into the cup of God's fury. (Revelation 14:9-10 NIV) What follows next is John is given a description of what hell includes. People there will be tormented with burning sulphur. The smoke of their torment will rise forever and ever. (Hell is forever.) No day or night will be there, never any rest for those who worship the Beast or his image, or anyone who takes the mark of the beast, 666. John calls those there to be patient despite the horrors ahead. Keep in mind what is in store for the fallen and the redeemed.

John hears a voice from heaven and is told to write it down. "Blessed are the dead who die in the Lord from now on." All dead are blessed, but those living through the Tribulation will be especially blessed. They will cease from their labor and their deeds are not unnoticed. They will follow them and be rewarded in the life to come. This is a promise to claim.

John looked and there before him was a white cloud and seated on the cloud was "One like the Son of Man" (a favorite description Jesus gave to Himself during His first coming). He had a crown of gold on His head, (no doubt Jesus) and had a sickle in His hand.

Then, another angel came out of the temple and called out to the King of Kings in a loud voice. He is the One sitting on the cloud. (Jesus) He was told to take His sickle and reap for the harvest of the earth was ripe (ready to be judged). So, the Lord swung His sickle over the earth and it was harvested.

What follows in verses 17-19 is two more angels appear, one from the temple in heaven and another who was in charge of the fire from the altar. The second, in a loud voice, told him to use the sickle and harvest the grapes, which were ripe and throw them into the great winepress of God's wrath. This is a preview of the world judgment to come to the world system that intoxicates people and they will be cut down and thrown into the winepress of God's wrath.

What is said in verse twenty predicts the Great War to come where the blood will flow rising as high as the horse's bridles for a distance of about 180 miles. No doubt blood could be splattered as high as a horse's bridle. But is it a river of blood covering the Holy Land? I cannot say. I leave it for you to decide.

15 REVELATION
The Last Seven Plagues

After having received a glimpse of what was to follow, John is given a vision of another great and marvelous sign in Heaven. Seven angels will be seen now finally with the last of the plagues. With them God's wrath will be completed. We saw seven seal judgments, the seven trumpet judgments, now we will see the fulfillment with the seven bowl judgments. These judgments will be more severe and more complete than the proceeding ones.

John sees what looks like a sea of glass with fire and those who had been victorious were standing beside it, much like the Israelites at the Red Sea, on the verge of being set free from their slavery to Egypt. These had refused the mark of the beast and to worship his image. They held harps given to them by God and sang the song of Moses, a servant of God, and the song of the Lamb. In Exodus 15, they had sung this song when they had been victorious over Pharaoh and Egypt. It was sung of God's faithfulness to the Israelites and the promise that Israel's enemies would be defeated. These were singing because finally justice would be delivered soon. It was a song of praise looking back at how God had delivered them through the blood of the Lamb.

John sees a temple in heaven, that is the tabernacle of testimony and it was opened. Out of it came seven angels with the seven last plagues. They were dressed in shining linen (denoting purity) with golden sashes around their chests (denoting royalty). They were on divine mission. One of the four living creatures gave to the seven angels, seven bowls, each receiving a bowl filled with the wrath of God. He is the eternal One who lives forever. The temple was filled with smoke from the glory of God and from His power. We remember each time Moses entered the tabernacle of God, God's glory came and a cloud would fill the temple. No one could enter this temple, until the seven plagues of the seven angels were completed. Hereafter, God speaks to each of the seven angels and tells them to pour out His wrath on the earth.

16 REVELATION
The Seven Bowl Judgments

Our God is such a God of mercy and compassion that mingled with each judgment; we see His love and care of people from all nations. (Discipline is a part of love.) Interjected between each of the judgments we see a pause, a delay to show how He cares for even sinners. It is hard for us to understand how many refuse His mercy and opportunities to be delivered, still to go on with their evil ways, even to the point of blaspheming and reflecting the marvelous atonement available. Everything about this chapter shows us that this is the most awful period in human history. We now see the horrendous final judgments in the form of seven bowls of God's wrath poured out on mankind. There is a warning here. Today is the day we must repent in order to avoid what is ahead. The fact that the Church has been Raptured, some are saved during the tribulation, and God has sealed His Jewish people doesn't give us much comfort, for evil is on the march and it is impossible for us to grasp just how evil man will become before God says, "No more delay, it is time."

A loud voice comes out of the temple and the first angel is told to pour his bowl out on the earth. Foul and loathsome sores came upon all men, all men but those set aside by God. If you have ever had to cope with a break out of boils, only then can you relate in a small way to this pain. Like the Israelites in Goshen when the Egyptians received the plagues, only those wearing the mark of the beast and who worshipped his image were affected.

When the second angel poured out his bowl on the sea, it became like the blood of a dead man. Every living creature in the sea died. In the second trumpet judgment, 1/3 of the sea was affected, (Rev. 8:8) but here, a total judgment, not just partial. When you stop and think of all the people of the earth who have a diet of mainly fish, you can appreciate the tragedy of this judgment.

The third angel poured out his bowl on all the rivers and all springs of fresh water, and they too became blood. The angel declared God was righteous in this judgment, because man had shed the blood of the prophets and given them blood to drink. They were receiving their just due. From the altar another angel said, "Even so, Lord God Almighty, true and just are Your judgments."

Another angel, the fourth, poured out his bowl on the sun and he received power to scorch men with fire. The result was rather than repent, they blasphemed the name of God, did not repent or give Him the glory. This is so hard to believe. To love your sin more than even avoiding the scorching heat is just so unimaginable. I can't even stand driving with the sun hitting my face from the side window it burns so bad.

The fifth angel pours out his bowl on the throne of the Beast and his kingdom became dark. They gnawed their tongues because of the pain and darkness, and sores, yet, they did not repent of their evil deeds. Now we see God intensifying His judgments due to their hardened hearts.

The sixth angel pours out his bowl and the Euphrates River dries up, so the way is prepared for the kings of the east with 200 million soldiers, plus others from eastern countries to pass on dry land. Already this is possible, and has been, since the Aswan Dam was built. God didn't need any help; He could and did so in the past before in the Old Testament times for Moses and the Israelites at the Red Sea, and for Joshua and the Israelites at the Jordan River. Three unclean spirits like frogs came out of the dragon (Satan), from the mouth of the Beast (Anti-Christ), and out of the mouth of the False Prophet. These demons are most likely not literal, but descriptive of the ugly evil these three personages of the counterfeit unholy spirit's power given them. They probably had the ability to move these evil people of the world with their powerful speech, like so many dictators before them have done. Included in this power will be the ability to perform miraculous signs. But they are no match for Almighty God. But they gather the whole world together for the battle of Armageddon.

Another warning re-iterated, "I am coming as a thief, blessed is he who watches and keeps his garment lest he walk naked and they see his shame." This represents being spiritually unprepared. A thief never calls you on the phone and tells you to be prepared as he will come at 2 a.m. and rob you. Nor will our Lord give these a warning to be prepared other than this for this horrible judgment.

The final angel, the seventh, pours out his bowl in the air. The number seven denotes completion, so this will complete the judgment of God. A voice came out of the temple of heaven from the throne accompanied by thunderings and lightnings; and a great earthquake such as not occurred since men were on the earth. When we think of some of the great earthquakes, we tremble and can hardly envision what this one will be like.

The Great City split in three parts. Many say it is Jerusalem, many believe it is Babylon. Whatever, it is the experience of God's fierceness and wrath. Not only them, but many of the world's great cities collapse. Every island disappeared and the mountains disappeared. (Think of how much evil had been committed in these.) Hail such as we have never seen fell. Each piece weighed about one-hundred pounds. Surely this brought men to repentance! No, they blasphemed God, because of the plague of the hail since the plague was very great. If you wonder how people reject the Lord in these days, and how evil this world has gotten so bad, think about these things.

17 REVELATION
The Scarlet Beast With the Woman Riding

The world has long used religion to work out its evil purposes. We have seen that the Anti-Christ is a Master at this, as he comes on the scene as a man of peace and deceives even Israel with his deception. He will use the False Prophet to set up a world-wide religious system and ends up using him to promote worship of himself, going so far as to require man to worship him in the Jewish temple itself. If we realize he is indwelt by Satan himself, this is not hard to believe. As I see evil in the world increase more and more, this is more and more believable as I get older.

When the Anti-Christ is finished using the False Prophet for his evil purposes, he will destroy him too. As we many times see in the Word, the Lord so often has the final say and His judgment is the real reason for the demise of Satan's plans. He uses evil to work out His purposes, as He did at Calvary. Satan thought he finally was destroying Jesus Christ and it was through that very destruction that our salvation and that of the world was worked out.

The following will be helpful as you read this chapter.

- ❖ HARLOT-PROSTITUTE: Counterfeit World Religious System
- ❖ BEAST: Anti-Christ-World Political Leader
- ❖ BABYLON: Political-Economic System of the Beast
- ❖ WATERS: Multitudes of People
- ❖ 7 KINGS: Five were Egypt, Assyria, Babylon, Persia and Greece and one is, and is to come… the Roman Empire.
- ❖ 10 HORNS: Ten Nations-a U.S. of Europe, EEC a fore-runner.
- ❖ BEAST: One of seven kings, but also the 8th. Head of the Revived Roman Empire.

One of the angels of the bowl judgments invites John to come and see and he would be shown the punishment of the prostitute (counterfeit world religious system) who reigns over and has control over many peoples, including their minds. The rulers of the earth and many inhabitants committed spiritual adultery with her. In fact, they had been intoxicated with the wine of her adulteries. If you have had dealings with those who were controlled by their intoxication from alcoholic beverages, or drugs, you know they couldn't get enough of them and they had lost total control of their reasoning powers.

The angel then carried John in the Spirit into a desert. There he saw a woman sitting on a scarlet beast that was covered with blasphemous names with seven heads and ten horns. She was dressed in purple and scarlet and was glittering with gold, precious stones, and pearls. All were symbols of riches and great wealth. In her hand was a golden cup filled with blasphemous names and the filth of her adulteries. In other words, this woman was as vile as the word itself. If we had any doubt who she was her name was written on her forehead in V.5, "Mystery Babylon the Great. The mother of prostitutes and of the abominations of the earth." This was none other than the World Religious System riding on the filth of her adulteries. The scarlet beast here was the political-economic system led by the Anti-Christ, indwelt by Satan himself and synonymous with the political system. This woman was drunk with the blood of the saints; their blood was a testimony of their refusal to worship the Beast, but rather Jesus Christ.

John was astonished with what he saw, and was given an explanation in V.8. The beast which you saw once (Roman power) was not (any longer a power), and will be, (the Revived Roman Empire of the last days, the demonic world political system led by the Beast.) He will come from the Abyss (Satan) and go to his destruction. All whose names were not written in the Lamb's book, (the saved of all time) will be completely astonished. We need a mind of wisdom to comprehend all this. The closer we get to this day, the clearer it will become.

John is also told the seven heads are the seven hills on which the woman sits and many think this is Rome, noted for its seven hills. (As many others think it is Babylon or some other city.) They are also seven kings (leaders) five have fallen, one is, and the other one is yet to come and must remain for a short time. The beast who once was and now is not is an eighth king (Revived Roman Empire) and belongs to, or comes from, the seven and is going on to his destruction.

The ten horns (powers) you saw are the ten kings (leaders) who have presently not received a kingdom but for one hour (a short time) will, along with the Beast. Their reason to exert and have this power is to yield it to the Anti-Christ who is one of the seven leaders in power. The angel further explained that the waters you saw where the prostitute sits (false world religion) are the multitudes from all nations and languages. The Beast having power from the ten powers, will show his true colors and he will hate the False Prophet and the false religious system and will bring them to ruin and will leave her naked (exposed and might even recognize by then the Anti-Christ's true identity.)

He will eat her flesh and burn her with fire (utterly destroy her). Remember, the world population will set him up as a God and blindly follow anything he says. If we read the last two verses, we see it is really God's purpose and has put it in man's hearts to fulfill all His words and purposes. The woman John is told again is the great city that rules even the kings of the earth. (A city like Washington often represents the U.S.A. because it is the center that makes all the political decisions, so is synonymous to the U.S.A.) The Beast is the savage ruler of that city which is synonymous with the world-political-economic system.

18 REVELATION
The Fall of Babylon the Great City of Power

An angel that had great authority came down from heaven and the earth was lit up from his splendor. He shouted with a mighty voice, "Fallen, Fallen is Babylon the Great." This was the worldwide evil personified political-economic empire headed by the Anti-Christ. John was also told "she has become a haunt for every evil spirit, and the haunt for every detestable bird." (Vultures, hawks and all sorts of birds of prey.) "For all the nations have drunk the maddening wine of her adulteries." (Drunk on power and every vile act imaginable) "The kings (rulers) of the earth committed adultery with her and the merchants of the earth grew rich from her excessive luxuries." (Not necessities, those who took the mark of the beast feasted in luxury, while they took advantage of the situation of Christians, even to the point of martyring them.)

Then, John heard another voice from heaven, God's voice, telling them to separate themselves from this evil world political system. Why? So you will not receive any of his plagues for her many sins, for there are so many there, they are piled up to heaven and God has not forgotten a one of her crimes. Give back to her a double for what she has done, including the torture and grief she gave to God's people and the glory and luxury she took on herself, for she boasted in her heart arrogantly and was full of self-centeredness.

She lived sumptuously, like a queen not like a widow (the poorest of those left behind.) The people actually believe they would never moan or answer to God; they were in absolute control of their own lives. But God said of her that in one day her plagues would overtake her, death, mourning, and famine. She will be consumed by fire, for despite her belief that nothing could touch her; the mighty Lord would judge her. The rulers of the earth, who also committed adultery with her, (physical and spiritual) as they shared in her luxury, would be judged.

When they saw her burning, they wept and mourned. Not out of pity, but they lost their livelihood because of this world collapse of their financial system. Terrified by her torment, they will stand off and cry. They had gone so far into materialism this was the result. They cried, "Woe, Woe O great city, O Babylon city of power!" In one hour (quickly) your doom has come. The merchants of the earth will weep and mourn over her because no one buys their cargoes anymore, gold, silver, precious gems, pearls, fine linen, purple, silk, and scarlet and all luxuries of food products, which were available to none but followers of the Anti-Christ. And we must not omit the bodies and souls of men. Slavery of all types were rampant, especially what we are seeing today in small amounts, human, sexual, and physical enslavement.

Never to be recovered will be the splendor and the cargoes thereof. The wealth gained from this will be gone. And they will stand off afar and weep, mourn, and cry out, "Woe! Woe O Great City, dressed in rich attire with glittering gold, precious stones, and pearls." In one hour such a great wealth has been brought to ruin. They truly thought it could never happen. Everything for them had been going so good. God has said, "Be sure your sins shall find you out," and this is the day. (Numbers 32:23b) All who have any connection with the seas, such as sea captains, those who travel by ships, sailors, and those who earn their living from the sea, will stand far off and exclaim, "Was there ever a city like this great city?" They will throw dust on their heads (signs of deep mourning). They will also weep, mourn, and cry out, "Woe! Woe, O great city where all who had ships in the sea became rich through her wealth." In one hour, (repeated to emphasize the suddenness of her demise) has been brought to ruin! God has finally passed judgment on her for the way she treated the saints, apostles, and prophets. Finally, rejoice, for God had avenged you for her evil.

A mighty angel picked up a boulder, the size of a millstone and threw it into the sea. With such violence, the great city of Babylon will be thrown down never to be found again. The harpists and musicians, flute players and trumpeters will never be heard in you again. (No more carefree parties or celebrations.) No more work-men in any trade will ever be found in you again. The sound of a millstone will never be heard in you again. The light of a lamp will never shine on you again. No more glad voice of a bridegroom and bride will ever be heard in you again.

Your merchants were the world's great men; by your magic spell all nations were led astray, NO MORE! In her was found the blood of prophets, and all the saints who have been killed on the earth. (These were all the many that refused to follow the Anti-Christ and False Prophet and the evil political-economic system and the false world religious system.)

19 REVELATION
The Great Praise Service

Revelation 4-18 dealt mainly with the events of the Tribulation. Now, beginning in chapter 19, we see a noticeable change. The Tribulation is coming to an end and the spotlight focuses on heaven and the Second Coming of Christ. This is a time of great rejoicing as we have just seen the destruction of the horrendous political-economic system of the Anti-Christ. Many had long awaited God's justice on this terrible system that caused such bitter torture, enslavement, and death to God's people. It is no wonder that after these things, what had just taken place in chapter 18, a loud chorus from a great multitude in heaven praising God was heard. "Alleluia! Salvation and glory and honor and power belong to the Lord our God! For true and righteous are His judgments, because He has judged the great harlot (World-wide religious system) who corrupted the earth with her fornication; (spiritual adulteries) and has avenged on her the blood of His servants shed by her. Again they said "Amen! Alleluia!"

The twenty four elders (representing the Old Testament and New Testament leadership) and the four living creatures, (symbolic of all creation) fell down and worshipped God who sat on the throne saying, "Amen! Alleluia!" Then a voice came from the throne saying, "Praise our God all you His servants and those who fear Him both small and great!" John heard the voice of a great multitude as the sound of many waters and as the sound of mighty thunderings, saying, "Alleluia! For the Lord our God Omnipotent (Unlimited Power) reigns." (This is in anticipation of the Second Coming of Christ. His reign was never in doubt.) Let us be glad and rejoice, give Him the glory, for the marriage of the Lamb has come and His wife (the church) has made herself ready." She was arrayed in fine linen, clean, and bright and the linen is the righteous acts of the saints. Saints are justified by grace through faith. These righteous acts are those done through the grace of God after salvation by grace.

John was told to "Write: 'Blessed are those who are called to the marriage supper of the Lamb!'" And He said to me, "These are the true sayings of God." Marriage is used to describe the relationship between Christ and the Church. Marriage in the First Century included three stages. **Phase 1** – Legal arrangement between two sets of parents, including payment of a dowry. **Phase 2** – the coming of the bridegroom to claim his bride. **Phase 3** – the Wedding Supper, a great celebration that lasted several days. The spiritual symbolism = **Phase 1** – Offers betrothal to all in the church age when each is saved, and Christ pays the price once and for all for His Bride. (Hebrews 7:27) **Phase 2** – Will be at the Rapture when the bridegroom comes to take His bride. **Phase 3** – Will take place at the beginning of the Millennium (Thousand –year reign) at the Marriage Supper of the Lamb (Jesus).

John was so overcome that he fell at the messengers' feet to worship him. But he was told he should not do that, for he was a fellow servant. He should rather worship God! For the testimony of Jesus is the spirit of prophecy. This book is all about the triune God, not about apocalyptic codes. The focus is always on Jesus Christ.

Then, beginning in verse 11 we see the Second Coming of Jesus Christ. (Not the Rapture, which happened between chapter 3 and 4. He never touched the earth, the Church was simply caught up to heaven, and then, the Tribulation occurred. He doesn't come as He did as a babe in the manger. He was born of a virgin mother to die as the Suffering Servant, as is recorded in Messianic Prophecy in the Old Testament. In Isaiah 53, we see He would be despised, a man of sorrows. He was wounded for our transgressions and buried for our iniquities to die so we could have eternal life, a flawless sacrifice, a substitute for all our sins. Now, He is coming not as a humble babe, but this time John sees heaven opened and a white horse and one who sat upon it called Faithful and True, in righteousness to judge and make war. His eyes were like a flame of fire, (signifying severe judgment) and on His head were many crowns (Ruler of the Universe). He was clothed in a robe that was dipped in blood, (symbolic of His sacrificial death). (II Corinthians 5:21) His name is called the Word of God. (The Living Word cannot be separated from the Written Word. They are one and the same.)

The armies of heaven clothed in fine linen, white and clean followed Him on white horses (Symbolic of purity, sinless perfection, the righteousness of God). This time out of His mouth goes a sharp sword, that with it He should strike the nations (The lost nations, judgment). No longer is He a man of peace, but a man of war. He will now, at this Second Coming, rule the world with a rod of iron (In absolute control, ruler of the world). He Himself, Jesus, treads the winepress of the fierceness and wrath of Almighty God. This is a dramatic vision of the awful judgment of God. This verifies the verse Hebrews 10:31, "It is a fearful thing to fall into the hands of the living God." He has on His robe and thigh a name written: "King of Kings, and Lord of Lords". An angel is seen standing in the sun, and calls for the birds that fly in the midst of heaven to "Come and gather together for the Supper of the Great God, that you may eat the flesh of kings, the flesh of captains, and the flesh of mighty men, the flesh of horses and those who sit on them and the flesh of all people, free and slave, both small and great." (All those who make war against Christ.)

And John saw the capture of the Beast, (The Anti-Christ, and evil world leader) with the False Prophet who worked signs in his presence, deceiving those who received the mark of the Beast and those who worshipped his image. These two were cast alive into the lake of fire, burning with brimstone. And the rest were killed with the sword, which proceeded from the mouth of Christ, (a simple word created the world, now a word of God sitting on the horse destroys.) All the birds (scavengers) were filled with their flesh. Though this makes us want to shout in praises, we will yet see Christ isn't through just yet.

20 REVELATION
The 1,000 Year Reign/The Great White Throne Judgment

Most students of the Bible believe that chapters which follow chapter 19 are chronological. We have seen Jesus at His Second Coming riding on a white horse. No longer is he a suffering servant, but the King of Kings and the Lord of Lords. Jesus defeats millions of the evil world system in a battle with the sword of His mouth. The armies of the earth are no match for the armies of God's Almighty power.

Then, beginning in chapter 20, we read that John saw an angel coming down from heaven, having the key to the bottomless pit with a great chain in his hand. He laid hold of the dragon (Satan) the serpent of old, who is the Devil and bound him for one thousand years, casting him in the bottomless pit, the Abyss, locked him up by setting a seal on him so he could not escape and deceive the nations no more till the thousand year reign (millennium) was over. After these things, he must be released for a little while. You see, that old Satan has always been on a leash by God Himself, and could only do as much harm as God permitted. With that harm, God always worked out His good. (Romans 8:28, 37-39) This Abyss was not the lake of fire, but the abode of the dead, waiting and locked up till the time when he would be set free again before the White Throne Judgment.

John sees thrones in heaven and those given authority to judge sat on them. The purpose of the millennium kingdom is to fulfill the promises made by God. Finally, God's kingdom on earth will be as it has been in heaven, as prayed for by His children for years. (Matthew 6:9-11) Martyred tribulation saints were before the thrones that had not worshipped the Beast or his image and had not received his mark on their foreheads or on their hands. They came to life again, and lived and reigned with Christ for one thousand years.

The rest of the wicked dead did not live again until the millennium was finished. This is the 1st resurrection. Christ was the first one to be resurrected (first fruits) with a new body. We know some others also were resurrected at that time. (Matthew 27:52-53) So how can this be the 1st resurrection? The 1st resurrection is used here for all the saved people in contrast with the 2nd resurrection, which followed the second death (Spiritual death). All the righteous take part in the 1st resurrection. The final resurrection (the wicked dead) takes place at the end of the millennium. Those who take part in the 1st resurrection are truly blessed. The second death has no power over them. They shall be priests of God and Christ and shall reign with Him.

After the millennium reign of Christ, Satan will be released from his prison in the Abyss. The earth has been repopulated during the thousand years and Satan goes out to deceive the nations over the earth, Gog and Magog to gather them to battle, their number being as the sand of the sea (numberless). A perfect environment and perfect government cannot produce a perfect heart. You have to say one thing in agreement, Satan never gives up trying… he is persistent. But his power is limited, and our Lord's is unlimited. He still wants to take God's throne. The battle was no contest. Fire came down and devoured them. The sole purpose was for the Lord to pass judgment on all who followed Satan. The devil who deceived them was cast in the lake of fire and brimstone, where the Beast (Anti-Christ) and False Prophet (false religious leader) reside. No comfort for them, as they will be tormented day and night forever and ever.

Then John saw a Great White Throne and Him who sat on it. God reigned in the beginning and He is still reigning at the end. The earth and heaven fled away. Undoubtedly, the Great White Throne was neither in heaven nor on earth, since both fled away. Who was sitting on the throne? Most likely, it is Christ Himself. (John 5:22-23) The dead, small, and great stood before God and the books were opened. It doesn't say which books besides the Book of Life, but surely God keeps a record of our sins. The Bible is a record of our need of salvation and records of the many chances we have had. There will probably be a record of the degrees of punishment, even a book that records our birth. Last but not least, will be the book containing the names of the redeemed people of the ages, the Book of Life. Only true believer's names are recorded there. The dead were judged by what was in them.

The sea gave up all dead in it, Death and Hades delivered up the dead in them. When each was judged by what their works showed, whether true faith that brought a changed life or not, all the lost were thrown into the lake of fire. This is the second death. If anyone's name was not written in the Book of Life, they were cast in the lake of fire.

Remember, this is a judgment for all those who have rejected God's love and sacrifice of His only begotten Son. (John 3:16) I will not ever have to face this judgment as I will either die or be raptured. I will only face the Judgment Seat of Christ for all those saved in the church age for rewards of righteous deeds we have done. Jesus paid the price in full for my sins at Calvary.(II Corinthians 5:21, Hebrews 7:27) If you have settled this, you also can take great comfort from this book, knowing God has done all He can do out of His love for you and I. God never sent anyone to hell. They chose, fully knowing what they were doing, to reject God's love and grace. (What man cannot do and only God can gift us with.)

21 REVELATION
The New Jerusalem

Following the thousand year reign in Chapter 20, John saw a new heaven and a new earth. This is not a restored heaven and earth, as the old had passed away. Though the present world we now live in is ¾ seas, we see there is no more sea in this new world. John sees the holy city, New Jerusalem, come down out of heaven from God, beautifully prepared as a bride adorned for her husband. Jesus said in John 14:2, "In my Father's house are many mansions; if it were not so, I would have told you. I go to prepare a place for you." This is that place Christ has been preparing for over two thousand years. Though the city is beautifully prepared, it is not the old Holy City Jerusalem. It is a heavenly city and doesn't have an earthly temple. The most important thing about this new city is now God dwells there. He is the tabernacle. And His Bride, all the children of God, will dwell in His presence and have perfect fellowship. He will dwell with them and He will wipe every tear from our eyes, and there will be no more mourning or pain, all that has passed away.

John was told to write this down for these words were true and faithful. This is why we have this book today. God wants us to know that when this time comes, it will be worth it all. Because John was faithful we know the end from the beginning, we have read this book left for us. God is all we need. He is everything from A to Z. He will satisfy every thirst, physical and spiritual. Overcomers have all this to look forward to. Can you even imagine what it will be like to never have to deal with an evil thought or deed again, for all evil will be forever in the lake of fire. Its residents, Satan, fallen angels, Anti-Christ, False Prophet, and those described in v.8.

Then, one of the seven angels who had the seven bowls filled with the seven last plagues came to John and said, "Come, I will show you the Bride, the Lamb's wife." He was carried away in the Spirit to a high mountain and shown the holy city Jerusalem descending out of heaven from God, filled with the glory of God. The only way John could describe her light was that it was like precious brilliant gemstones. Things that men sold their souls for, what they stole for, fought for, are common building materials in this great city and it was all a part of the gift and promises kept by the Lord God to us as overcomers. We will gain it all. Matthew 6:33, "But seek first the kingdom of God and His righteousness, and all these things shall be added to you."

This heavenly city had twelve gates each made of one solid pearl, named after the twelve tribes of the children of Israel. The wall of the city had twelve foundations and on them were the names of the twelve apostles of the Lamb. The height, width, and length of the city was about 1,400 miles. An angel stood guard at each gate. (Ezekiel 48:31-35 elaborates on these gates of the city.) Since the twelve foundations of the city are named after the apostles and the gates represent Israel, both Israel and the Church will be in this city. The dimensions include a high wall of 1,400 miles in height and is 216 feet thick. The city was approximately 1,400 miles square. This is about ¾ the size of the U.S.A.

The construction of its wall was jasper, like a clear diamond and was pure gold, as glass. It was adorned with all types of precious gems. The twelve gates, as I said, were made of twelve perfect pearls. How can we even imagine such a city as this? The streets were paved with pure gold. What a glorious city! No temple was needed for the Lord Almighty and the Lamb is its temple. There was no need of the sun, or moon to shine in it for God's glory will illumine it. The Lamb is its light!

Its gates will never be shut as there will be no need there, for it will never be without light. We will all have access to God. Sin will be gone forever. Never will we have to endure sin again. Where will the lost be? As we said before, they will eternally be in the lake of fire created for Satan and his fallen angels, and all those who followed them will be there. We will forever enjoy this utopia that men tried to possess all their lives here on earth. All because we accepted God's free gift of salvation and looked forward to the promise of eternal life. This revelation given to John shows us the glorious future for those who put their faith and trust in the living, giving God.

22 REVELATION

The End Is Coming/Last Invitation/Last Warning/Last Promise

As we approach the end of the book of the Revelation of Jesus Christ, hopefully we realize this is just the beginning of eternal life. Daniel was told to seal up his book till the end, (Daniel 12:9) but

John was told not to seal up his book. (Revelation 22:10) There is a most important reason for us to simply understand what is coming in the end. We need to be prepared, we need to be sure family and friends are prepared, and we must proclaim that the world needs to be prepared, for it will come quickly. Many Christians, me included, believe we are near the Rapture of the Church. If we interpret the times, according to the state of the world right now, we know for a certainty, it is imminent.

Let us read this last chapter and ask our Mighty God to reveal to us what He wants us to simply understand from this final, yet most important chapter. Remember, this book was written not to confuse, but to reveal things soon to take place. God has shown His sovereignty by erasing ALL evil from this new world. The final battle is over, the Millennium is over, the Great White Throne Judgment of the lost of the ages is over, Satan, the Anti-Christ, fallen angels are gone, and the False Prophet and all who rejected Jesus as Lord have been thrown into the Lake of Fire and brimstone by their own choice. Now, we will see a further glimpse of the city of New Jerusalem and what is in store for us.

John saw a pure river of water of life, clear as crystal coming from the throne of the Lamb (Jesus). This was symbolic of the holiness and purity of the city and God who resides in this city. In the middle of the street, and on either side of the river, was the Tree of Life, which Adam and Eve were forbidden to eat in the Garden of Eden. Here we find it yielded its fruit every month and those in the city were not forbidden to eat. In fact, this tree was therapeutic, as the fruit and leaves contributed to their good health. There were no more curses, for all evil has been banished forever.

We will live in intimacy and closeness to God and the Lamb, as we note here we will see His face and we will belong to Him. (His name will be on their foreheads.) New Jerusalem will not have a temple, as the city itself will be the temple. The throne of God will be there. Our highest joy will be that we will reign with Him and serve Him forever and ever. These words we are told are faithful and true. God sent His angel to show us what will shortly take place. Again Jesus says, "Behold, I am coming quickly! Blessed is he who keeps the words of the prophecy of this book." This book is not the imagination of John. It is a picture of God's love, truth, and faithfulness.

John was so awestruck by what the angel showed him that again, he fell down to worship the angel. The angel told John absolutely not to do this, only God was to be worshipped. Then, he told John not to seal the words of the prophecy of this book for the time is at hand. If the time was short then, think of how short it is today. The angel added that those who didn't heed this prophecy would continue in their wickedness and those who were righteous would continue to be righteousness. If any hadn't heeded his words, they wouldn't no matter what. (That is a fact!)

Again in verse 12, Jesus repeated the fact that He was coming quickly and was the Alpha and Omega (First and last letter of the Greek alphabet, the Beginning and the End) the First and the Last. He would reward accordingly. He issued a blessing in verse 14 of those who do His commandments. They have the right to eat of the Tree of Life (eternal salvation). They would also have the right to enter the New Jerusalem (Heaven). All others (the lost) he itemizes in verse 15 would remain outside, lost forever, outside of God's love.

Jesus certifies that He is the One who authorized His angel to testify of these things to the churches. He was the true Author, the Root, and the Offspring of David, the Bright and Morning Star. He offers a final invitation in verse 17. The Spirit and the Bride say "Come!" And let him who hears say, "Come!" And let him who thirsts come. Whoever desires let him take the water of life freely. (Paid in full for by the death of Jesus Christ once and for all on the cross at Calvary.)

The Last Warning is also given in verse 18 to anyone who hears the words of this prophecy and would add or subtract to the prophecies of this book. His name shall be taken away from the Book of Life, from the Holy City and what is written in this book. One of the things people hate is that Christians are exclusive, we hold to the words of this whole Bible as our final say in all matters of faith and practice. We are exclusive, because God is very exclusive. There is only one way to be saved and we must cling to that.

Jesus gives a Final Promise found in verse 20. He who testifies of these things says, "Surely, I come quickly." To this John gave these words, "Amen. Even so come Lord Jesus." This is John's final prayer. And it is ours. Amen means "I agree". A final benediction is given. The grace of our Lord Jesus Christ be with you all. Amen! As the book began, so it ended. It spoke of the revelation of Jesus Christ and what would take place very soon. Jesus is coming soon, and it will happen very quickly. Today is the time to settle that matter and open your heart and let Jesus in. Confess, repent of all your sins, ask Jesus to be the ruler of your life, and then you will be ready for this great occurrence when it comes. My prayer is that you will be ready. You will have no excuse if you are not ready. God bless!

About the Author

Theresa J. Royal was born and reared in Willimansett, Massachusetts. She graduated from Chicopee High School where she took Secretary training. Terri, as she is affectionately known, met and married her husband Jim who was in the Air Force and became a beautician. After her husband retired from the Air Force, she became a pastor's wife for 24 years. Both she and her husband did voluntary mission work for eleven years in Kino Bay, Sonora, Mexico. Terri has spent forty years teaching, and still teaches Ladies Bible studies.

Other books by Theresa J. Royal

SIMPLY PUT

Practical Biblical Application for all our Life

THERESA J. ROYAL

Other books by Theresa J. Royal

SIMPLY
DEVOTIONS

DAILY SPIRITUAL
RENEWAL FOR LIVING

THERESA J. ROYAL